Wild Bo Rabbit Takes the Pie 🥧

JOCEY GREEN & JEAN GREEN

To order additional copies of this book, contact:
Xlibris
844-714-8691
www.Xlibris.com
Orders@Xlibris.com

ISBN: Softcover   978-1-6698-4827-1
                  EBook   978-1-6698-4826-4

Print information available on the last page

Rev. date: 09/23/2022

To my mother,
A worshipper

Deep, deep, far into the woods, if you ever had the opportunity to happen upon a colorful family of animal inhabitants, you would find an especially vibrant little bunny named Wild Bo Rabbit.

Mr. and Mrs. Rabbit's home was nestled far into the pines, and the small town they lived in was called Piney Temple Wood.

So many lovely things surrounded their home. Vines hung, and leaves of various hues from great trees fell from the roof and past the windows. There were lots of foliage for the children to play in.

Wild Bo's mother—her name was Anna Bell—made the most delicious pies you ever had the good fortune to eat.

Everyone loved Anna Bell's pies, but Wild Bo loved them best of all. It didn't matter if Wild Bo was all the way by the High Falls; he would race upstream along the river to get home to that pie. This is also how he got his reputation of being the fastest bunny in the forest.

His father, Charles Ottis, was out in his garden. Resting on his knees, he pulled the weeds out of the earth that threatened to suffocate his little flowers. With slugs and caterpillars, there was a whole life inside that garden that his father loved. Wild Bo held all the color and temperament of his father; they were very much alike, and he and Anna Bell loved Wild Bo very much.

The house was very busy. Mamma had her hair pulled back in a big bunny beehive. She was smiling real big with rouse painted lips into some gleaming pots and pans. There was to be a pie-baking contest, and Anna Bell was whipping up her finest one—a delicious pie with a crust that cracked open just enough to let a little steam out with glimmering sugar on top. That was her Pastor's favorite so she made it every year for the competition.

Anna Bell had grabbed an egg and cracked it, letting the gooey sun middle slip into a mixing bowl.

"Oh, my stars!" she said. "We are fresh out of carrots. Son, would you go out back to your father's garden and check if there are any new carrots ready to be pulled."

The backyard is where the vegetables were, one of two gardens his father Otis poured his time into and took great ownership in.

"Yes, Mama," he said. Hopping outside.

"No carrots here. I see mustard greens, purple cabbage, and squash!" he hollered to Anna Bell through the window. "Can you use any of these?"

"I most certainly cannot," his mama said, wiping her hands on her apron. "I will have to send you out to the market. Now go get more carrots and sugar, and be quick about it."

With a flash, Wild Bo Rabbit had zoomed all the way to the market and had come back with the supplies she requested. Anna Bell gave her son a kiss on the cheek for returning quicker than she expected.

"I really do think you might just be the fastest little bunny in all of Piney Temple," she said with a laugh.

Quickly, Mama began putting all the ingredients together, and before you know it, she was pulling her renowned pie out of the oven.

Opening up the curtains, she let the light and cool air from outside wash over the pie that was placed on the windowsill. A wonderful aroma of cardamom and spices moved all about the home.

Everything seemed to be going according to schedule, she thought.

Walking out of the kitchen, Mama went upstairs. She swept the hallway, dusted the cobwebs, and folded the laundry.

All of Mama's cleaning was done, and when she went back to the kitchen, she found that her pie was missing!

Who in the world would have taken her pie, she thought. She looked around the kitchen for it. Maybe one of her children came in and moved it. But no, she couldn't find it anywhere.

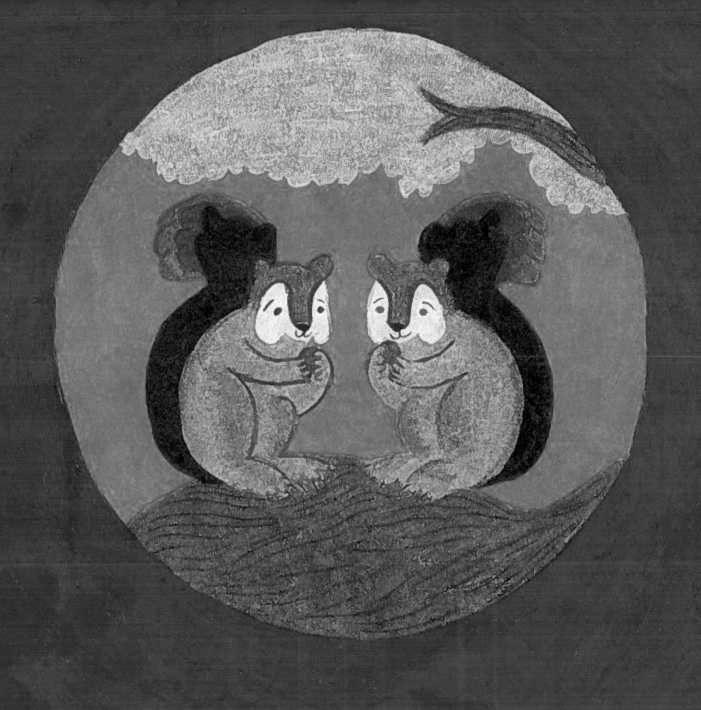

Edgar Bee and Eddie Lee, two identical-looking squirrels, had raced up a tree. One was holding an acorn, and the other was struggling to grab it.

Wild Bo had come running from his house, sending waves of wiggles across a great fern patch that surrounded the tree they were in.

"My, look how fast Wild Bo Rabbit is racing off down that trail. I wonder where he's headed this time," commented Eddie Lee.

They had watched him earlier on his way to the market to get supplies. But where could he be going this time, they thought.

"Looks to have his hands full," remarked Edgar Bee, and resuming their child's play, they raced down the pine and off into the dappled sunlight.

Now as faithfully as the moon would find night and the sun would find morning, dusk was dawning, and it began to grow dark. Wild Bo's mother was concerned, not only because her pie had gone missing, but also because now her child was missing too. *Goodness gracious, where is my boy?* she thought. Wild Bo knows better than to stay out this late!

The townspeople were alerted and grouped into search parties. "We will look from up high, Mama Bell," said Edgar Bee and Eddie Lee, the two bushy-tailed squirrels.

Charles Otis, Anna Bell, and their other children, whose names were Jazzy, Johnny, Joshua, and Jo searched down low in every nook and cranny of the forest floor. A veil of lighting bugs was brightening their way. Anna Bell refused to fall into worry but instead prayed and held on to faith that her baby would turn up.

Edgar Bee and Eddie Lee found Wild Bo's tracks and followed them. They were determined to find their friend and knew a place he might be. Wild Bo went to visit the High Falls often. He loved to run by the great plummeting water. He liked to see his reflection racing alongside him as he ran. Little bunny footprints led them to the waterfalls, and there they saw a bunny sniffling in the moonlight. He was scared and covered in pie.

"Wild Bo is that you?" they called out, a little scared themselves.

They had never been out past nightfall, and they missed their parents and their cozy beds that were waiting for them back at their tree house.

"Who's there?" Wild Bo cried out timidly.

"It's us, your friends Edgar Bee and Eddie Lee. The whole town is looking for you. What are you doing here?" they asked.

"I did something bad, and I'm too ashamed to go home," Wild Bo said in tears.

"I stole my mama's pie and ate it all, and she's going to be rightfully mad at me. She will never want me to come home now. I'll have to live with a stomachache in the forest forever. Mama might forgive me when I get to be an old bunny, but until then, I'd have to stay here all alone," he sobbed.

23

A branch cracked off in the distance, and an owl with big yellow eyes hooted. The noises frightened them! Edgar Bee and Eddie Lee hugged their friend tightly.

"You have gotten yourself into a heap of trouble now, haven't you, Wild Bo? But it's not true, your Mama loves you very much. She is looking for you right now, along with your Papa and your brothers and sisters. We better get home."

"Okay," said Wild Bo. "I'll never steal Mama's pie ever again."

One very sticky bunny and his two friends began their journey back. "Take it easy on us," said Edgar Bee. "We don't have the speed to keep up with you, Wild Bo."

"Oh, don't worry," he replied. "I am going to take things much slower now. I am going to think about what I do before I act, and I'm not just going to put my feet out ahead of myself," he said with a laugh.

He could see his home now; all the lamps were on inside. Charles Otis, seeing him hop onto the lawn, dropped what he was holding and ran to meet him, crushing one of his prized vegetables. "Papa," he said, "you've squished one of your squashes!"

Embracing his little bunny, Papa said, "Nothing is more important to me than my family."

Anna Bell and his brothers and sisters hopped up to greet him.

"Mama," he cried, hanging from her arms.

"Well, thank goodness you're back and safe," she said, kissing him all over. She didn't even ask about the pie.

Instead, she said after squeezing him real tight, "I think you better say thank you and good night to all the townspeople. You'll be needing your rest for your apology in the morning."

"You mean you're not mad, Mama!" Wild Bo said with a surprise.

Mama explained, "I'm not mad but disappointed that you'd think you had to run away from home because you made a mistake. Everything in this home, you are welcome to if you'd ask for it.

Your father and I love you and your brothers and sisters very much. Now because you did not ask and took something that did not belong to you without permission, you will be getting disciplined. We discipline you because we love you. But I would never want you to run away, Wild Bo, we would miss you too much."

Mama then put him in the bath and cleaned off all the sticky pie and scrubbed between his floppy ears.

"I love you, Mama," he said with a fresh set of tears. "But what will you do about your pie for the contest?" he asked.

"Oh, I borrowed some ingredients from our neighbor earlier this afternoon, enough to make a pie for the competition and one great big pie for all of us," she said, and she kissed him again.

Mama grabbed a big warm towel off the counter and wrapped Wild Bo inside. She picked out his favorite pajamas, the ones with polka dots on it, from his dresser drawer and laid them on his bed. Getting dressed, he slipped into his nice crisp sheets, and his mother pulled the blankets up to his ears just how he liked. He heard a knock at the door, and Jazzy, Johnny, Joshua, and Jo came in and fell at his bedside.

"We're so glad you are home," said one.

"We looked all over for you," said the other.

"I knew he would come back the whole time," said the youngest. "I wasn't worried at all."

"Enough," said father, walking in to the doorway. "It's time for bed. Say good night."

All the siblings piled in for one last hug, saying, "We love you."

"The fair is tomorrow!" they exclaimed. "We can't wait!"

That night Wild Bo thanked the Lord for his loving family, his church, his pastor, and all the townspeople who had been out looking for him, and he went to sleep. He knew he never had to hide anything from his parents because they loved him. He would never take things without asking again.

The End.

Printed in the United States
by Baker & Taylor Publisher Services